SO-FJB-013

The Poet's Domain

Volume 38

Find the Heart of the Metropolis

Wider Perspectives Publishing ¤ 2024 ¤ Hampton Roads, Va.

Copyright December 2024, Hampton Roads, Virginia
Wider Perspectives Publishing – J. Scott Wilson

Poetry and Writings herein are products of the authors listed with those works and all rights to those works revert to the authors at the time of 2nd run/release of this volume. Authors are therefor responsible for distribution and withholding of their works after such time and should be contacted for permission before any repackaging, reproduction, or recirculating of their pieces. Permission granted by one author does not translate to permissions over any other authors' works and the individual authors shall have final control in resubmitting their own work beyond this volume to contests or other anthologies after 2024.

If you are unable to order this book from your local bookseller, then please contact the publisher directly.
HRACandWPP@outlook.com

With immense appreciation to Pat Adler & Live Wire Press, and to the Poetry Society of Virginia and Virginia Writer's Guild

Anne Emerson's Beautiful Arrogance, or a version of it, has been accepted for publication in *NoVA Bards 2024,* Local Gems. Sept. 11, 2024
Leslie N. Sinclair's War Story First published in the PSV Centennial Anthology, 2023

The Poet's Domain
Vol. 38 copyright Hampton Roads, Va. December 2024
Find the Heart of the Metropolis
ISBN: 978-1-964531-98-4 var2. 979-8-309967-49-0

Foreword

I was asked to write a foreword to this volume, and I find the "preview" poems much in keeping with my worldview. So I will tell it like I see it. James can always edit out the more provocative remarks, or even write his own

In my experience, when people at the upper echelons of the socioeconomic strata misbehave or shirk their duties, the people at the bottom die. Or, if they don't die, they become stunted, emotionally or physically or both. On the other hand, people at the upper echelons fail to become all that they can be, because it is too easy for them to misbehave or to shirk their duties! I will not quote Jesus at you, but if you are a Christian, you should be familiar with what Jesus said about the rich man.

There are poems in this volume about how it feels to be a Hebrew dying in the Holocaust, or at least, how to be a surviving relative exploring the idea. There are poems about how it feels to have to live in a city slum where the landlord doesn't care for the housing; about how it feels to see money spent on something glamorous and sexy instead of something needed; about how we – and other creatures of nature - adapt to city life, where good food doesn't grow, so we have to beg, steal, or cheat for poisoned crumbs.

There are also poems about redemption – how to choose another path; even about how to walk into the jaws of death with your head held high. Someone said we should watch the works of poets and artists, if we wish to measure the pulse of a culture. I agree with that; but I don't see a solution to their angst in these pages. I challenge all you poets to find a way to read these poems aloud to – and engage – your friends in high places. Perhaps they don't know that you suffer; or perhaps they care so much that they don't want to see. It may be that only in our old age do most of us, or even only some of us, gain the courage to look the devil in the eye.

Anne Emerson (a twin, like Elvis, the Great Communicator; and a spare, like Prince Harry, because I am the younger twin - or so they tell me.)

Contents

Foreword
by Anne Emerson

Contributor's Prize

Contributor Bios

450 East 81 Street, NYC

Joan Casey

Garlic, onion, cabbage
smells of different nationalities
seeped under metal doors
and filled the five-flight walkup
until replaced by sudsy ammonia
some Saturdays.

When summer made walls sweat,
we hung out on the fire escape
gulping air filled with blares from
emergency sirens, car horns, pop and rock.

Our apartment was on the first floor
above the dry cleaning store.
Each super lived next to us before he was fired
and the next one hired. Police always banged
on the super's door to end drunken brawls, no heat, or
water backing out of toilets from a board
stuffed in a drain years ago.

Garbage cans lived and bred under the stairwell,
where I hid one day to escape a gang.
There were no trees on our block
but grass grew in cement cracks
that I jumped over as a child –
not to break my mother's back.

My brother and I shared a room big enough for two
cots. We moved. The neighborhood was gentrified.
That building remains, now with
two trees in front, and our apartment
still over a dry cleaners, renting for $3000 a month.
Blinds on the super's place hang crooked and broken.

Coaldale, Pennsylvania

An elegy for a town on Highway 209,
120 miles from Manhattan

We follow the hearse with my uncle's body
for the customary last ride
past his small house once home to generations.
As with other occupied houses on the street,
mowed grass covers the big back yards
once filled with vegetable patches, chicken coops, shanties,
and washtubs.

We drive by one of the town's four closed-up churches
whose parishioners once boosted buying
exquisite stained-glass windows,
imported from Austria,
with their miner's pay.
Boards cover the holes
left in the brick.

Our cortege continues along a wall
enclosing the school yard.
You can only imagine children's voices.
We pass what was the supermarket
that sold poppy seed ground to order,
a five-and-dime store long without its sign,
and a cardboard ice cream cone standing
in a dusty window of the once drug store
that sold vanilla ice cream cones
topped with chocolate, marshmallow, and crushed peanuts.

3

The ride is short.
The town is small.
When number eight breaker shut down,
not even a fast-food chain moved in.
We head out on Water Street
past houses that sunk into ground,
past the bus stop shelter where a sign still reads:
EVERYBODY'S GOAL
IS MINE MORE COAL.

New York, New York:
the Native's Return

Ageless drag queen of the night,
home to consummate wealth and lethal poverty,
lure for millions who would dare dream
of exceeding even in destruction.
An anomaly, always a contradiction in terms,
like change immutably caught in still life.

Destination to visitors from just-named nations,
provider for denizens in diverse ghettos,
you whose arteries smell of roasted chestnuts in icy wind
and flesh baked on heat-drenched cement,
how dare you, after so many years,
awaken my spirit?

I finalized our divorce after raising my inner child
and traded time-evaporating sensations for tranquility
to nurture seeds in new soil
until clinging tendrils weakened the aging trellis.
Now, you deliver me of memory's debris
and clear road to soul.

Here, in the place to come for dreams
I find feelings to take me home.

The Stalked

It comes at the same time every morning –
while we breakfast –
appearing out of nowhere,
moving with a mission,
taking guard one foot to the left of the oak,
with tail prone, pointing at us,
it sits for hours.
Sometimes an ear twitches.

No neighbor claims ownership.
It's gray feral feline
well fed,
never seen capturing its prey.

We sip coffee,
exchange glances at it,
at each other,
at articles in the newspaper.

Investigations continue
man shot to death by police
taxes up, interest down
cheaper hernia operation in Germany
snow, earthquake
mudslides, floods
tornados, fires

and the cat still sits
while we unravel like yarn
ready to be pounced on.

Sunday Afternoon at the Docks

On a tugboat at South Street,
New York City

They come like cats for the smell of fish
or the sound of sour salt wind in their hair.
They grow light rocking on a weathered tug
throwing their wrappers and cans to the sea,
but soon tire of the breathing
and leave,
tired
tanned
and tense
through the cemetery
to their tall grey coffins
who await them.
And all the while the sun slips through the arms of the sea
kissing it goodnight,
until after dark
when there's only the sound of an old sea captain
dancing with an ancient hound
in the wind.
and in a
far
dark corner,
one cat cries.

We the People, in July 2014

"The Wealth of Nations" by Adam Smith
and The U. S. Declaration of Independence
were both written in 1776. Both were
revolutionary manifestos challenging
the abusive alliance of state
and corporate power.

Our founding fathers,
those males of certain races,
who could pay poll taxes
gathered in the humid
fly-infested city of brotherly love
in 1787 to secretly declare their birth right
as citizens known as *we the people.*

> A corporation's right to personhood
> was given legal recognition in 1819
> in the case of Dartmouth College *v.* Woodward.

We the people was revised
when men of all races, colors,
or previous condition of servitude
became *we the people.*

> The court refused to hear further argument about
> personhood of corporations. No doubt remained
> about corporations being *we the people.*

Doubt remained about women being people
and those who couldn't pay poll taxes

and how old you had to be
to be *we the people.*

When all *we the people* were granted personhood,
the question arose about which
we the people could vote *v.* just influence the vote.

    Some voters gathered
    under Montana's big skies
    to allow all who had personhood
    to vote.

The argument was:
"Corporations are people, my friend,"
Corporations are *we the people.*

    The voices of *we the people*
    with dark money grew louder and louder.

The question remains:
who are we the people?

Beautiful Arrogance

Anne Emerson

My sword is silver, jeweled, etched, and loved,
with blade so sharp – precision-honed to kill.
The hand that wields it – elegantly gloved,
well-trained and deft – has fierce, determined will.

My word's enchanting, musical, and kind –
its message deep, portentous; pointed too.
The mind that writes it – daintily refined –
could craft cathedrals out of morning dew.

They're fully beautified, these tools of war –
designed and finished bright; maintained with pride.
I'm aiming not to need them anymore;
my rivals soon will join the righteous side.

Of course, I will not over-rule the grand,
nor use, myself, the beauty in my hand.

About Free Speech

Leslie N. Sinclair

To speak or not to speak, what is the answer?
Whether 'tis better for the heart to talk
of sins and sorrows and egregious things,
or pick a fight to dominate and crush them!

Some among us Do, while others Think.
Some among us Act, while others Talk;
Perhaps the Doers don't articulate;
or Thinkers don't participate – enough.

My parents taught me how to kill an insult:
"Words will never hurt me." Lies; they lied –
their posturing, provocative – it worked!
And so, we half-believe it; pass it on.

But here's the truth, for you observant ones:
"Sticks and stones will break my bones; bad words
will always hurt me." I walked away; I left
alone; until I had nowhere to go.

And when you have nowhere for you, what then?
My parents didn't tell me that –
they were the Doers and the Walkers. Go within;
or else to nature; now I speak – it's free!

Scheherazade (or her Sister)

Tiger Tiger pulsing bright
with the fire of the night,
caught in web of silver light
for waxing, waning Turk's Delight.

Who is spider; who a fly?
Which is truth, and which a lie?
Desert tent or palace high –
shall I live, or shall I die?

You believe you pull my strings;
I think you're right – you take my things.
You have shared your golden rings;
so pretty, but to me they're blings.

Everyone is watching you –
too rapt to notice I'm here too.

War Story

While grown-ups fought, elected leaders tried
to send their children far away from fear.
Your Granny didn't write this down; we pried
it from long-buried depths; so, listen, dear:

"Those aunties in the country wouldn't see
as Mummy saw; she brought us back to war,
where bombers flew to airplane factory,
and dumped their excess pay-loads at our door.

One night – with sirens wailing – breaking sleep,
we scrambled out to shelter underground.
An earthquake, from no fault-line, thundered deep
so close that Mummy blanched: 'That's our house, downed.'

Not ours – but opposite, the rubble lay.
It buried Dave and drove his kin away."

Workers Unnoticed,
a.k.a. "Critter Poems,"

I.   It Sensed my Intent

A cockroach was walking about
the floor in my bathroom at home.
I watched as it moseyed along
exploring its own little world.
But who wants a cockroach in-house?

The moment arrived when I thought,
I've watched it enough, now attack!
I moved not a finger nor toe,
there wasn't the time to do that;
it shot like a bullet, and hid.

II.   What Was it Waiting For?

A critter whose name I don't know
lay drowning before me today.
A small one, I'll throw on the deck –
a handful of water withal –
I don't want its feet on my palm.

But this was too big not to touch,
nor would it hop free of my hand.
I let it relax there awhile
and flutter the wet off its wings,
but still, it would not walk away.

I took myself out of the pool —
perhaps a hard edge isn't kind
to two-inch green critters with wings —
and offered it leaf after leaf
in planter pots next to the wall.

It stayed on my hand, even backed
away from the flowers and leaves,
then started to walk up my arm.
While wondering what it might need,
I thought to step out of the gate —

no shoes, with my swimsuit for clothes —
then place it to nibble "my" plants;
but that didn't happen because
it sensed my assistance and crept
to freedom on palm frond at last.

III.   What did it Need from Me?

I rescued a critter today,
descending, apparently gone.
It didn't fall free of my hand —
its stiff little leg seemed to move
so slightly I wasn't quite sure.

I waited but it wouldn't budge,
nor did I step out of the pool,
because I'd be waiting too long.

I walked with it, taking my steps;
not swimming, for then it would drown.

I wondered what this one would teach,
then focused on nature around,
not self or the bug anymore;
and that's when it seemed to revive.
It left me but wouldn't stay safe.

Departing the pool, I looked back
to see how it managed itself.
I wanted to find it a plant,
and thought, from within, to provide;
and that's when it crawled from the edge.

IV.   Why Didn't it Take its Bellyful?

I sat on my rocking-chair porch;
a hummingbird came to say Hi,
and butterflies I hadn't known
to live in my yard fluttered by.
Surrounded by noises of life,
the world as my backdrop, I read.

I felt a mosquito jab in;
decided to let it alone –
not brush it away; swat it dead;
nor even react at the red
that swelled up its little behind.
Another came by; took its take…

I watched them, it seemed a long time –
enough for their bellies to fill.
A third one alit on my hand.
I noted the time, as I read,
but thirty secs later it's gone –
it didn't have time to fill up.

I knew they had drunk by the itch
in spots where they'd punctured my hand.
I said to myself, never mind;
allow them a drink, tell the itch
it isn't required to be there;
and next thing I knew, it was gone.

V. Two Years Later

I got to the pool with the sun –
the earliest light of the day.
A critter was swirling, entrapped;
perhaps it had already drowned –
Another bug, giant and green.
Reviving itself at my touch,
it fluttered its wings right away.

I talk to them now, and I said,
"I think you can leave me to swim -
you don't have to walk, you can fly
away from my hand any time."
Perhaps it had wings that were wet,

or somehow its feelers were hurt.
It wouldn't depart; as the one,
two years ago, stayed on my hand.

I walked with it, watching it act;
Its legs were exploring my hand;
its mandibles nibbled me too.
It didn't seem sick, and I thought
"It's checking me out for itself,
ignoring that I want to swim."

I told it I had to get on;
I offered it leaves, but no way.
My fingers took hold of it next –
it didn't like that, to be sure,
but next time I tried, it fell off;
I left it there safe on a wall.

City Sinking

Serena Fusek

Under the waves
that scrabble and claw
at the city's walls,
under the waves
that—in the glow
of the ancient sun--
gleam like tarnished diamonds,
glitter like glass
gone radioactive
at a frequency
almost audible--

under the waves
into which the city sinks
like a woman
sleepy with opium
sliding under
the scummy bubbles
of her bath

waves that swallow
cellars, ballrooms,
infamous bedrooms:

no need to imagine
what lies submerged
under waves

sluggish with sludge
steeped in a millennium's muck

every high tide
laps above
the penultimate stain
fouling the stones.
Soon what skulks
under the waves
will slither through
city streets.

Every City Has One

I've never seen him.
No one in the city has
but below the sidewalk
beneath the cellars and
subways down in the slime
and slops and black water
of the sewers swims the
alligator: twelve feet
(or fifteen or twenty-five--
who holds a tape measure
to a nightmare?) of slag-
gray armor   of giant jaws
jagged with teeth
and a tail that smashes bones
with one sweep.

He was a kid's pet
 (the legend says) flushed
when he outgrew cute
and he continues to grow
in the darkness. By
touch and temperature
and the way the air flows
he glides through tunnels
and the water barely
ripples. He lairs in a section
so old it's lost from city maps

and rules the system--
the stench   the dripping bricks
the lost wedding bands glittering
in the muck the roaches
the sleek rats
and the spider
who weaves webs of delicate lace over
his clumsy head--

Sometimes a huge darkness
crowds the fenced outflow pipe
when he tries to reach the sun.

Interrogation

Between the Head that plans
and the Hands that build
there must be a mediator
and that is the Heart.

Adage from the movie, Metropolis

But what kind of heart
rests between?

Is it a heart
hate-twisted
as a thorn-tipped brier?

Is it a heart
tightly curled on itself
with the pain of a wound
that will not heal?

Is it a heart
like a house
with all doors closed
all windows shuttered?

Could it be a heart
voracious as the giant
who drank the sea dry?

A heart wild
and destructive
as a forest fire

or sluggish
as a river in drought?

Is it as polluted
as an ancient sewer?

Is there any heart
I could trust to mediate?
I'm not sure
I would trust
my own.

Pigeon and Peregrine

After the lock down
the protests
losses too many to tally
many buildings in the city
stand hollow as
played-out mines   holes
like empty eye-sockets
where windows were.
One has become a dovecote--
pigeons perch on the sills
strut court emerge from windows
like bees from the hive.
Their cooing hums
through the street.

The sun's first rays
glitter on the river.
The creamy brown hen
steps from the dark
of the building
to the sill   launches,
the flutter of her wings
silk on silk.

From the tallest buildings
(narrow slits of black glass
in walls like ancient stone)

something plummets   long
wings eclipsing
the rising light.   Talons
sink into down.

As quick as that
the hen's day ends
and mine begins
with her death
behind my eyes.

Rats, Rats, Hundreds of Coffee Loving Rats

*(from a video on the news of a rat carrying
a coffee cup along a NY subway platform)*

Why is that rat
carrying a paper coffee cup in its teeth
as he skitters along the subway platform?

Don't you know
in a city with a coffee shop
on every corner
the rats have become
caffeine fiends?

One rat prefers hazelnut,
the cute little girl rat loves French vanilla,
and that big one
standing on its hind legs
glaring at you
likes his coffee black
as a starless night sky.
He's nibbling the cup
trying to wring out
every drop.

 Baby rats ingest caffeine
in their mother's milk
grow up fast
alert
and smarter than

the average rodent.
In the glitter of their red eyes
staring at you from the shadows
their bright brains burn.

City Envy

Chris The Poetic
Genius Green

My rural Gloucester on the altar of financial worship
Altered by the need to expand
Who guides the hand of our future
Changing land of mine
I can't remember your design
Will I be out of line with your changing shape?
The image you replace
Of my hometown
How I see greed in operation
How I see you ask for cooperation
As you feed corporations
New foundations
For businesses we don't need
But the right hands were greased
How you only tolerate change when the right amount is exchanged
Hate how I see how the land change
How more buildings rise
How new homes are created, the ones born and raised can't afford
How you pretend to be sword and cut through middle…
Class
Hope to impress the rich
Think it will enrich
Our home
How you've been a metropolis it will take a superman to save
I love your country ways
Hate your city ambition
How you wanna industrialize

The beauty in front of my eyes
I hope you never block the sky
From my view
See the stars in your eyes
I hope you won't take them out of mine
Hope you don't lose your identity
I'm not asking you not to grow, just don't fall victim of envy
Of the city

Country Loving a City Girl

I loved her like the country fields we ran through
The black southern hospitality we were taught to uphold
Loved her like the food that fed our souls on the sunniest of
Sundays
Hated, how she was always gone
Child of the city, only replaced skyscrapers for trees when with me
1 weekend out the year
Always told me she'd miss seeing the stars
I missed the way her eyes lit up at night
Always compared them to constellations
words I wished I said like revelations
When she was out of sight
On flight
To a world out of my reach
I'm just a country boy
Never hailed a taxi
The smell of factories and smog
Sat on my chest like logs
I only knew grass and logs
Tire swings
And sweet tea
She knew city lights and late night
Gatherings on the Southside
Where girls were track runners
Momma told me I wasn't up to that girls speed
But I loved her
Like bike rides through abandoned corn fields

And honeysuckles
Loved her like grass stains on my play clothes
One time I held her so close I thought we'd fuse
She was always amused
At my thoughts of her being my muse
And we'd paint this countryside the brightest hues the good lord
got in his pallet
But the only challenge I could never win
Was how to keep her here
How to get her to ignore the city's call
To catch lightning bugs with me and remain my brightest light
To not trade the moonlight
For city lights
To not keep seeing past these trees
And plant roots with me

Literally Literature

Tripping off imagination
Falling into creativity
Trying to separate from feelings
Emotions in captivity
These bars are bars that imprison me
Lock me away from trauma I must face
Avoid my story in stories I create
Can't dissect my character, I'm in character
The plot thickens, the plot twisted
Using my brain to escape mental prison
Using my hands with surgical precision
Write poems I can live in
Cut out tension,
From reality
If poetry is therapy, the heart the mediator
I cover ears to mine
Until the doctor's notes reach the mind
advice taken like pills popping
My diction prescription to save my timeline
Without the heart I'm out of sync
Without emotions I'm out of ink
Literally I'm a literary puzzle I must solve
Can't have paper thin resolve
My fate,
is to be in control of the life I create

Beyond the page
The world's the stage

Physiology

Desires of the heart control the head
Use your hands to redirect the mind
Connect the lines to open a link to the divine
Palms pressed
When I grip the pen it's a prayer request
Decipher the emotions that lead me
Find the stories that need me
My mind a book of seals
Unlock thought
Creation is a gift for the spirit to shift
Mind. Body. Soul
From the crown to the sole
Gotta move with intention
Build a life with my tongue
I speak with invention
Lyrical intuition
Feel the words guide me
Words speak life, use mine to align me

The head is a hospital
The hands are surgery
The heart the mediator
God the psychology
Now that's physiology

Organic organisms orchestra of living
I break open this ink
Pen bending
Fccl this
If your heart willing
I spill for you
Open quill for you

Fly verse with this fly verse

I spill for you
Open quill for you

Fly verse with this fly verse

What Is It

Old Soul Poet

What is it that puts you above me
That I am lesser and beneath
Through no fault of my own
That I will live and die
Unknown

To only know darkness
Having only heard about light
A story passed along
From generations ago
Anonymously

I have only known this life
Is there more above here
Is this all there is
The spirit of hope
Nevermore

Is an extended hand enough
Will it be received
Is there not one
Among those above
Benevolence

What is it that puts them over us
Are they full of hate
Or are we guilty too
To divide ourselves
Eternally

Fallow

Lilli Reine

Owing to Him, I spoke soft words
To respond when hardness was predicted
What did it prosper?
A tenderness in humanity
A divine repair of two souls

In His sight, I walked away
Though lured to run toward
Where did it get me?
To a refuge of consciousness
A reprieve from the mental minefield

For His name's sake, I chose love
Not the reticent version that has no true hold on a heart,
From which I can easily slip away
Or the version that slides on the surface
Into the soft corners
No, I chose the love that requires tireless, timeless work,
That walks through the middle of each battle
Penetrating, when at all possible
Mankind's fallow ground
And for what?
For the perpetual rejection?
For broken places that flood with tears?
If not, then why?

I chose love because He first loved me
Because once
I, too, was fallow ground

Slithering in Slumber

Hey you
Up there
    I'm tracking you
    spying through the slits
    listening between the lines
    hankering voraciously

I see you
Traipsing
    lauding your reflection
    in the polished apples
    your trophy wife
    orders in the heirloom bowl

You look
Good
    to your brood
    who tell you they love you
    and believe the same of you
    rote words make hapless habits

Tell yourself you're not my kind
    you don't even know you're mine
    working for Nikes, sashimi, HOA fees
    working too hard
    yes, twice hard

Provider, sure
But protector?
>sowing seeds of truth
>vigilant against evil
>>creeping in through the cracks
>>slipping in unsuspectingly
>>messing with brood-ing minds

What do you suppose they do?
>when you're not around
>when you're too tired to be involved
>too disinterested to listen
>when the screen has seduced you to Neverland

I am
Greed
>with an insatiable appetite
>for never enough
>I want an infidel's delights
>I'm here for yours

Be afraid,
Be very afraid
>I plan to rattle your windows
>demolish your doors
>usurp your utopia

Go ahead
Be my guest
      rest your darting eyes
      fold your fitful hands
      sleep a fool's slumber
      while I slither beneath your floorboards

I'll let myself in, thank you.

Snatch

The birds are bickering
Dismal songs slam the skies
The doves disappeared long ago
Awful cries seep out through the crags
Natural fledging gave way on that last good day
Gave up the ghost to aberrant snatches and screeches

Last night
In the abysmal hour
Neighbor 665 screamed to her death
Swaddler 2665 — her last
Was snatched away
Just like her
First

> *a warrior*
> *for the coming*
> *harrowing*

Our days are counted and we are numbered
I can't dig deep enough into my brow
To dislodge this evil betrayer
I'm certain I'll be next
Can't end it now
I am needed
One day
More

CeCe

Shanya Lady S

There was a faint smell of bleach
Below students called my name
In the corners of the marble steps
You could see bugs and dirt from years past
All the students wanted something:
A snack, mental health break from calculus
But not Cece
She simply asked that I do nothing
So I asked for permission to acknowledge her
And she agreed
"Cece" I called out through the crowd
I smiled and she smiled back
The students often asked how she knew me
Why did the mental health counselor know her name
But we never told her secrets
Cece had so many reasons to see me
But never once opted in to this momentary relief
She just participated in our morning ritual
A ritual so pure, so beautiful and so innocent.
You can imagine my surprise
      when I told all my clients and referrals I was leaving
      and Cece cried out, "Who will smile at me now?"
      she asked "Who will treat me normal?"
That was the moment my heart broke into 1000 pieces
Leaving hundreds behind in a city that both built me
      and broke me
I hope that one days she understands

My smile was slowly disappearing in the city
I was once again caught in the fast paced vigor.
An appetite for corner stores and violence
        eventually wears away on the cheek bones
I had to leave before the city stole my smile once again
Dear Cece,
I used to be you,
With a smile that can be seen through the smog of the city
But now you are the reason I smile
I leave now to preserve this smile
I bring with me the idea that you can live through this
That you, too, can survive the city
But I will never stop smiling at you
I will never stop treating you normal
I will just smile at you from a distance
But please know there is room for you outside of the city lights
In places that you are more than a shadow
I just hope you get out before the city steals your smile

City Bird

I know you heard the story of the city mouse and the country
mouse
But have you ever heard the story of the country bird
     and the city bird?
The country bird builds a nest made of twigs and leaves
gently covered in moss for keeping babies safe
But the city bird builds nest on top of rooves, awnings,
     fascia and gutters
       makes nest out of paper, cotton clothing cut from last
       night's victim in the city.
Maybe she's just a vixen
       there's no wrong in the city.
In the country, the early bird gets the worm
But in the city, the evening bird finds old pretzels, breadcrumbs,
     Bojangles, and Popeyes
The city bird may look like a pigeon or a bluejay,
       but for the day old chicken, it will turn vulture
       cannibalistic not because they hate chickens
       or love feasting on their own kind,
       but eating a foul becomes a source of survival
In the country, baby birds tumble out of nest
       to find overgrown grass at their base
       at bottom of trees, worms under their feet
       even if they are hurt they can eat
In the city, baby birds tumble to find forest entry into Vasca turns,
       fatal sharp edges, cutting them open
       before they hit the hot concrete

When faced with fight or flight country birds
        often find refuge in the next tree,
Yet in the city, when mama birds are faced with fight or fight,
        they turn fighter jet faster than a bullet
        more deadly than a gun.
Mama birds shoot cannons in the city
        because when given the option to fight or fly,
        there is no option, they choose survival.
City birds don't just migrate they turn into multi-role flying drones
        appearing as needed, taking deep cover and
        protecting nations under her wings
Moving at speeds once unthinkable
Those who seem impossible to touch can easily be annihilated
And those once vulnerable become untouchable nestled
        under the sweet protection of city lights
The best city birds transform back into birds
        looking like pigeons or blue jays flying amongst trees,
        but please don't give them an ultimatum because
        you may just find their ability to transform

Deep Underground
A Paranoid Android Totally Recalls
Dreaming of Electric Sheep

Lisette Lorenz

According to the mechanistic view of the multiverse,
aren't we "human"—of flesh, bone, and ever-angst,
not those very in/organic automatons who,
having become painfully aware of their
own fully-automated existence,
RrRrRRaaaAge_against
@TheMachine?

Dream State

Crickyt J. Expression

"Blue. Everything was blue."
The hue draped over the town
like a gentle wave,
twinkling streetlights
mimicking bubbles.

Cars, traveling slowly
along double yellow divided rows
like armored fish;
traffic lights bobbing in the current-
bright granules of food.

Landscaping rocks- gravel;
City Park pines reaching skyward,
waving, resembling kelp,
azalea bushes mirroring coral.

Canting my head,
just woke from a nap,
    Am I still dreaming?
Swell propelled, I surfaced on a rock;
azure film gone.

Sea salt washed out of my eyes,
as delicate fingertips traced scale patterns
on my flowing tail, where once legs had been.

Slumber Magic had worked its wiles!
From my perch upon stone,
recalling Eriksen's Copenhagen statue,
I laughed and fancied myself
modern art.

(a Pg 36 Poem Prompt: 1ˢᵗ line of poem is last line on Page 36:
Book: The Next Person You Meet In Heaven by Mitch Albom)

Echoes Through the Veil

In the dark room of my head.
two years passed,

your absence curled over snippets of
memories
like yellowing edges of time worn
photographs,
blurred frames of over exposed
negatives.

Through glassy, dilated pupils,
in the stillness
I came to understand-

You aren't in the Darkness.

The echo of your voice is found
in the Light of Hope,
seeking
a better tomorrow,
a kinder populous,
a more arts focused public.

That is where we commune with you,
keeping your flame alive.

Everybody Knows

Ken Sutton

Everybody knows that
a flush beats a straight,
three of a kind
beat two pair,

and nothing beats
a 1911 .45,
hammer back,
safety thumbed off.

As a good American he learned young,
playing his older sisters and brothers
for bottle caps and buckeyes,
later, pennies and afternoon chores.

By fourth grade he'd graduated
from one eyed jacks and deuces wild.
Folding seven card stud with no bet
if the first three dealt failed to produce

a pair, two to a flush or straight.
Never glanced twice at a hole card
except to mislead. Showed doubt
only when he needed to goad a bet.

The gun came later.

Saturday Morning Drive By in Norfolk

From this bench I can tell the
approaching Mustang parks outside.
Pollen mars its bright ebony finish,
trapped by the damp from last night's rain
baked into place by the bright morning.

He's slow in his U-turn, taking his time,
and all of the intersection.
A low slung driver, his premeditated slouch
attempting the low rider gangsta affect.

Armor All gleams the sun back at me.
The treads whisper when he cuts the wheel
hard against the crown of 35th Street,
keeping well clear of the shallow groove
slicing across Newport Avenue,
carrying the rain's remnants
through storm drains to the Lafayette River.

Staring from behind wrap around shades
on his second slow circling
his mirror masked expression might be anger,
resentment at an out of place intruder.
Hardly idle curiosity. Idle is one pass, not two.

He's no junkie, looking for a mark to roll
and feed his disease, stabilize his day.

The Poet's Domain

A heroin addict will get up early,
if the sickness wakes him and forces him outside.
But no street junkie drives that kind of money.

Not a dealer, or even a dealer's shorty,
monitoring the hood for rivals or narcs.
Saturday morning doesn't exist in their world.
They hear about it on television
and wonder what it's like.

On his third circuit he drops his reflecting mask
just enough to expose a predatory glare.
I don't think he likes me.
I'm beginning to not like him.

Song of the Mugger

They tell me I am old,
that the level ground
lies uneven beneath my feet,
and for this, I carry a cane.

Slim, black, lacquered ebony
shod in hard dark rubber,
it holds the pavement firm
against the damps slick intent.

It's the crown they notice,
a sterling serpent, S shaped,
heavily scaled for surety of grip.
It nudges greed forward,

with it weight of worth,
balances the tip, bored hollow,
filled with lead and malice.
Balances the knife waved

by the nervous young man
who demands my money.
He eyes my cane's silver head,
will want it after he has my wallet.

Knife and wallet fill his hands.
He looks up at the whistling,
down at the dropping knife,
has not yet felt the broken wrist.

I spin and the cane whistles again,
slams into his neck, crushing his carotid.
I step back. He does not understand
why he is falling and never will.

After fishing his pockets for cash
I pluck him of two rings, but leave his chain.
Nothing that big and flashy is gold.
When I was young I had to find my prey.

Tookie's Blues

It's hard after struttin'. Runnin' the hood.
Watchin' old thugs and young bloods
cross the street to stay outta the way
of a man who did hard time at sixteen.

Who's not afraid to do it again.
A man who'll put em in the ground,
take their woman and make her like it
over one dollar short, one word out of line.

After all that, it's hard to know I was never
nuthin' but the dog with the longest chain.
Just another mutt to be pulled up short
and put down with a stainless steel needle.

Cor Cordium, Heart of Hearts

Tammy Tillotson

Do you think your mind powerful
like a turning machine?
Turn it off, now, dear.
Come to bed.
Tonight, your eyes
dance.

The Divine Mediations

I. Prelude for the Head

Yes, someone has to stay at the machine.
As every tortuous endless hour
Provides such plethora of steady power,
Wherein each fitted cog churns in between.
Does the end of work justify the mean?
If discord is sown and serves to devour,
Where a soul oppressed can only cower
To work below with a heart jaded-green.
When the whistle blows it's sleep or eat lunch
For its well-greased gears are highly practiced.
Rough sketches plan a pick-pocketed hunch
As these sweet minutes tick by the fastest.
Steady the rhythm which seeks to embed
The steady routine inside of one's head.

II. Intermezzo for the Hands

On a mid-day word search yet to be ink,
I once happened upon a mole kingsnake.
Along the path I had chosen to take,
Disrupting the train of thought I could think.
As fear did erupt, a steady stride break.
A flickering tongue, a glaring eye blink.
The rise in my chest was soon quick to sink,
In spying such yellow-bellied scale ache.
To feel warmth of sun on glistening rock,
To quench some dying thirst in morning dew,

61

To view this mirror, this image, to walk
Along the same path the Devil slipped through.
Where the reflection seldom understands,
Why shadows can not be grasped in our hands.

III. Furioso for the Heart

Might an eye belie the look on a face?
Should one be able to tell the difference,
Wielding a surface masked by ignorance
From the catacombs to a higher place?
Would the deepest depth of memory trace
through such ethereal effervescence?
Or keep an appearance of eloquence—
little children, fold hands, bow heads, say grace.
For I have come to you for sound advice.
For as you have called me, so here I am.
Yet of the seven deadly cardinal vice,
Do seek the truth, never wrath of a lamb.
While sins in a heap may not soon depart,
Feet can still move, still a beating man's heart.

Every Body is a Crooked Man

every Body is a crooked man
who walks a crooked mile
pursues a crooked livelihood
each crooked gear turns crooked pile
mews, crooked cat
woof, crooked dog
a crooked mind is but a cog

Metropolis Dizain

While powerful seems a turning machine
the hands that would build it know nothing of brains
that dream the dreams the heart has not yet seen.
As all the world holds to the devil's chains
seven deadliest sins, Death entertains.
Yet to be dismissed surely means to go
to depths where Hel knows the bowels below.
Where one man's curse is another man's praise,
of concentric shells in this Inferno—
what good are the plans heaped into mass graves?

No. 11811

concentric
shells
to return to the machine is to forget
brothers
sisters

Back to the Possibilities

Terra Leigh

I moved back to the city
After college.

A girl free from mountains
Of obligations,
I longed to come
Back home.

Now,
Nothing looks like
I remember.

I get lost here often,

Stare at the spotlights
Of ideas,
The shops full of passions
I'm not sure if I
Should indulge in.

I park myself in the middle,

Convenience myself
With all my needs,

Easy access
To my thoughts,

Beliefs,
A walk away
From new experiences.

I pass people
Indulging in their ideals,
Making names for themselves
In cafes of dreams,

And they make space for me
To try new drinks,
New creations.

I wander in and out
Of alleyways and parks,
Finding all the projects
I loved to play in,
Old and weathered but
Waiting to continue our games.

I look up into the sky,
And this city's dazzling lights
Can't overcast
The stars of possibilities.

The Brain/the Mind

J. Scott Wilson

I do not see through emotional eyes
I dress them in lenses logical
I am analytical
You say that's impossible
And you find my fabric cynical
I tell you I do better clinical

Hunger lies not in the stomach, throat or mouth
Love lies not in the heart
Hate lies not in the fist nor the face
You're looking for them all in the wrong part
It is the brain that holds them all
But to it's shame see how the brain deflects all the blame

Bringing it Around is Bringing Us Down/
The River

There is a river that flows
It flows through the life of each
For those at the end it's a trickle
But flow widens, and ends up depositing a beach

And this river has flowed for some time
But not as long as you'd think
Twenty-nine hundred years ago in Phoenicia
Man first hungered for this metal drink

But in this group, in this land
Bringing it around is bringing us down
And ugly green bike moved from auction to auction
Until it sits in a shop here in downtown

So go our choices, so go our lives
So goes the tip of this mount of ice
At the bottom of this economy you move about in remnants
Forget the variety, forget about spice

We're just a part of the crap redistribution plan
Put some cheap plastic in a trailer in San Diego
Tractor trailers play leap frog all day and all night
Move around until they occupy a parking lot in Ohio

Then somehow this ice jam at the mouth
Sends the headwater and overflow of wealth
But instead of sand bags that keep the river within its banks
Their levees keep waters close, keep up a sense of health

Our great crap redistribution plan
Is gladly brought to you by "Da Man"
Bringing it around is bringing us down
Take one down, pass it around
We can rest assured with the knowledge
That he learned this rule in college
That when the party has over One-Oh-One
That there will be no beer left over for some
Get used to hearing that, too…
"There's just nothing here for you"
Unless you count emotions and situations
Which occupy all your motivations
And taken down and passed around
With interest on annual compound
Until the child is slammed
With the sins of the parent, be damned!

But the river flows no matter who owes who
Long ago it's mechanics were put into motion
And those who more-than-drank from the middle
Are assured their fill despite any commotion

So the money flows in straight lines
And the water's high behind each dam
But bringing the spares around is knocking us down
And really leaves the world without a plan.

Cold Cries Pass Between Us

My level, your level
and the crying girl two floors down
all trigger each other
and we push it around.

What stings you, kills me
but we don't make a sound
And we sit here afraid of what
has driven her keel aground

Racking, sobbing her echoes
beckon like freezing pain
Silent, think our fears pale
bring us a little shame

We couldn't hear her sorrow
Until we ran out of knives
Her sounds pass between us
Now that we look back at our lives

With pursed lip and sad eye
look at your hand
I want to take it to hold it
say I'm not like her man

Sorry I called your pain petty
since surely made it worse

We were both just responding
until we discovered her curse

I hope we're thinking the same things
about each others fraying edge
that we neither want the other to be her
draped on the window's ledge

Maybe she weeps for us
first-timer peace that we shattered
At what level did she finally break?
Is that really what matters?

Discontented America

We work ourselves into a foam
Trying to comfortize our homes
In debt to our eyes
Placating credit with our lies
Then we're driven to our cars
Seeking refuge near and far
We know we're not going somewhere
Except back home to sit and stare
Because deep in our hollow hearts
We may as well be seeking stars

Let Up on Flint

If I were to be technical
When steel meets flint hard enough you create a spark
When lead meets the Flint water supply you kill off the spark for a
generation or two

See if you thought I was joking
Then you would think I was tasteless
Unlike the flavor of contaminated water
The governor of Michigan says he'll personally taste the water
from Flint every day for a month
But I am aware that Flint has at least two kinds of neighborhoods
And in some the water, post personal filter, is probably good

And all he is saying is that they fixed the problem now
After that damage was done anyhow
But why are any of you sticking up for Flint anyway
What I mean by that is – why did you just start today

Flint, Michigan has been under the gun for longer
       than many of you've been alive.
See that town's troubles started when GM jobs went overseas
       and Flint's job scene died
While '80s America boomed the Republican recession
       started there.
Who knew that a little town like Flint
       would be 15 years ahead on the trends

And so were you around when Iraq War recruiters
       made the military the only job in town
What patriotism did to Bedford, Va in World War Two
Poverty did to Flint starting in 2002

Progressions and Diverging Points

They move here
I don't care the reasons, it matters little
It is the order of things in this country
They bring renewal
Those who oppose them enjoy the gathering of stale air
     about themselves
They move into apartments, some swanky   some slums
They get jobs through connections
In cities they network through their ethnicity
Some are pretty or handsome, or they aren't
They move up in their jobs, or they don't
They move on to single family homes, or they don't
They find love and companionship and forge families,
     or they don't
I feel sorry for the ones who don't
Their bosses didn't promise them top positions
No one teaches the hustle and the drive and the will
No one even promises love, except the lovers
Wait and see if it works, or they don't

I moved there
Not such a big leap, except of faith
I thought I was following the order of things
You promised love, you were a lover
That was like a renewal of each of our spirits
Few opposed save those stinking of jealousy

We moved into slum, happy to store our hearts
      in each other's swank
You were my connection to a job, I slid into the network
Together, we were our own ethnicity
We found each other's best looking parts
You made job advances through my labors
You looked into improving junk into homes,
      dreaming of my lucridity
But you denied me opportunities, said success lay in your path
You turned my companionship into a singularity and
      decorated with hidden rage
You isolated yourself from your family
I ignored, misinterpreted signs
You isolated me from family, my own history
You forced family upon me, but froze my interaction
You got defiant when I feel abused, or you didn't
Your own children wore the clothes of neglect, or didn't
You treated my children with kindness, or you didn't
You avoided grocery shopping, or you didn't
You kept leaving the house with the wrong list, or you didn't
Maladaptive coping strategies
You kept every loving promise you made, or you didn't
You took responsibility for your actions and improved,
      or you didn't
I waited to see if you could at least devise a plan
      for love to survive
           And you didn't.

I moved to the homeland
Even that became a leap of faith
I moved into swanky accommodations, or slum
Divorce is the order of things in this country
I seek renewal, but practice habits.
I worked a year and half to mend my children
Their American dreams still take nights off
In their bad nights you come to take their dad away
I practice strategies that work, or they don't
But we keep things fresh, like ocean air
My children and I are the base unit – without fail
We are beautiful to each other – without fail
We are kind to each other – without fail
We keep promises to each other – without fail
I refuse to let one kind of love supplant the promised
      – without fail
I flail about at finding companionship – without fail
I became sickly and worn out like age, I cook and eat better
I fought bronchitis, hypoxia and syncope, and smoking
      – without fail
I gained depression weight, I joined a gym
I distract easily like PTSD, I forge ahead
I form networks and friendships, advancement comes slowly
I write poetry to convince myself that I can do it,
      that I will make it
Or I don't
      I will survive you
         Or I won't.

Holding Court

Rabbi Israel
Zoberman

I regularly hold court at my neighborhood Starbucks
In the City of Virginia Beach,
with all the coffee schmooze lovers
Invited to join the lively conversation of the day's news
From multitude perspectives as equals with often
Me the only Jewish presence.
Before the earth turned heartless, my great grandpa,
Rabbi Yankale of Zamosc, had starry mournful deep
Eyes of exile and a wavy red beard with stuck crumbs
Of bread and mouthful blessings from faithful lips
To feed the throngs of hanging children hungry
For both satisfying flour and living *Torah* verses.
At the Belzec death camp the Rabbi held his last earthly
Court among disciples and fellow inmates till summoned
By his impatient executioners to move up to a higher realm
Where he hurriedly ordered the Most High to be brought
By the ministering angels to testify on the fate of those
Pure Jewish children swallowed by inexplicable hatred.
Soon enough the Holy One was found wanting and my
Agonizingly daring great grandpa – even more than Father
Abraham- banished his Great Friend from the heartless
Heavens in the name of love.

Remember to vote for your favorite poem in the volume

The POET'S DOMAIN

Acknowledges

The poem

by

as being selected as the

favored or best poem

by a majority of votes
from contributors to volume

Meet the Poets
of vol.38 ...

Contact Points, Biographies, "Bios", Pointers, Accomplishments,
Publications, Favorites, Discussion Points...

Anne Emerson is incorrigibly interested in everything, including other cultures and peoples. She likes to work with her hands, and also spends hours in thought – ideas running off in many directions. Her friend, Nannette Hoffman, taught her to write poetry as a form of healing, after she experienced emotional distress at the age of thirty-nine. Nannette encouraged spare use of words, and experimenting with different forms and styles. Anne became active in two poetry workshops and a photography club. She was born and raised in England, immigrated to the U.S. with her DC-born husband on 7-7-77, lived in the DC area for forty-one years, and retired to Williamsburg, Virginia in 2018. Anne's poems have been published in NOVA Bards, the Poet's Domain, and a PSV publication. She has presented poetry (her own and others') to senior communities in Reston and Williamsburg. Anne's address for any correspondence, is: PO Box 701, Williamsburg, Virginia 23187.

Joan Ellen Casey started writing poetry at age twelve, but living frequently got in the way. After working as an editor for New York publishers, trekking through South America alone as a twenty-five year old female, raising a family, earning a doctorate from William & Mary, teaching, and writing educational materials, she quit to concentrate on writing poetry. The first poem she submitted for consideration won the Metrorail Public Art Project Award from the Poetry Society of Virginia. Since then she has been published in many volumes of The Poet's Domain, seven other anthologies, and has contributed to the Poetry Society of Virginia's Newsletter.

Serena Fusek lives in Newport News with her husband where she is known as a somewhat eccentric cat lady. She has three full length collections of poetry: Alphabet of Foxes (San Francisco Bay Press), Ancient Maps and a Tarot Pack (Bitter Oleander Press) and Heartwood Dreams of Blossoms (Wider Perspectives

Publishing). She recently retired from teaching poetry at CNU's Life Long Learning Society to work on her fourth book.

Chris "The Poetic Genius" Green is a thirty-eight year-old poet from Gloucester, Virginia. For twenty-four years, The Poetic Genius has been working to perfect his craft, using it to empower himself and his community through poems exploring his African American heritage, his family history, and his own life experiences. He is the 2023 winner of the PSV's Honoring Fatherhood award for "Breaking Myth," a poem about the misconceptions of black fatherhood, and 2nd place winner of the Golden Nib (Chesapeake Bay chapter) for "Morph," a poem about the perils of drug life and the need for drug abuse aid. The Poetic Genius is a board member of Slam Connection, a nonprofit organization out of Williamsburg, Virginia using poetry to uplift the community through workshops, open mics, and outreach. He is also a member of the Chesapeake Bay Writers. Through his efforts, The Poetic Genius hopes to bring about change to this world and inspire others to do the same .

George Barry Hamann aka G Barry aka **Old Soul Poet** was born April 27, 1965, in Rochester, New York. When he was five, his family moved to the nearby town of Victor where he graduated from Victor Senior High School in 1983. He earned his bachelor's degree from S.U.N.Y. at Geneseo and later received a second degree with honors in Mortuary Science from Gupton-Jones College of Mortuary Science in Atlanta, Georgia. George also recently became a Certified Funeral Celebrant. He currently lives in Poquoson, Virginia where he works as a licensed funeral director. Old Soul's passion for writing started in his early years and that passion has never faded. He often shares his "Thoughts for the Day" on his Facebook page entitled "Old Soul Poet" created in 2013. He has also self-published three compilations titled Reflection of an Old Soul vol I, II, and III available on Amazon.

Lissette Lorenz creates speculative fabulations at the intersection of art, science, and the environment. Their work can be found in Art + Media: Journal of Art and Media Studies, JCOM : Journal of Science Communication, and Objet-a Creative Studio's BECOMING trilogy. Using mixed media, they blend poetry, prose, zine-making, and collage to explore themes of Earthly un/worlding during times of planetary transition. Lissette was born and raised in Miami, Florida, a bioregion that has been transformed from Everglades wetland to teetering metropolis. A child of Latin American immigrants fleeing war and poverty, they grew up somewhere between princess-like Disney World fantasies and complicated post-colonial realities. They also lived in Tokyo, New York City, and New Orleans before settling in Virginia Beach with their partner and many, many plants. Find more at lissettelorenz.com.

Crickyt J. Expression A Baltimore Native, now calling Hampton Roads her home, Crickyt J. Meyer performs her poetry on stages as C.J. Expression. Spinning wisdom into whimsy, playing with words as toys, she creates messages ranging from fanciful imaginings to attacks on social injustice. No topic is taboo. Often speckled throughout her work are life lessons, in hopes others may glean from her words the warning or encouragement they need to find joy and be better humans; especially to one another. You can find her healing poetry collection Dear Broken Woman: Trials to Triumph through Wider Perspectives Publishing or by directly messaging her on Facebook. Seek C.J. on socials: FB: C.j. X. Pression or IG: @crickytseye

Early-years' travels, her faith, an inter-racial marriage, and three decades of mentoring young women bolster **Lilli Reine**'s depository of thoughts and perspectives. A former seminary and law school student, Lilli's works often probe the search and struggle for redemption. Her poetry and prose have been published in Vita Brevis and Scarlett Leaf Review

Leslie Sinclair loves life, and the world. Trained, many years ago, as an economist, but unable to swing the compromises required for a career in the fast lane, she finds current economic challenges demanding of engagement from the perspective of one who has lived as an immigrant, full-time mother, and low-paid part-time worker. Her poetic preference is for the lyrical, but more recently her thoughts on the natural world and some of what is being portrayed in the media have also found their way into her poems. Her poems have been published in the annual anthologies, NoVA Bards and The Poets Domain; also, in the PSV Centennial Anthology.

Ken Sutton is not crazy. But he does have voices in his head, old men and children, friends and enemies, close relatives and people who waited with him at a bus stop in 1966. They have something to say, an act to justify, a sorrow to share, a moment of awe that overcame them in the event and still does in memory. He has two books out, Manhattan to Machipongo and The Convenience of War. He will be bringing Here in Downtown Machipongo out soon and Water from a Bitter Well is nearing completion.

Tammy Tillotson lives and writes in Chase City, Virginia. She is a member of the Poetry Society of Virginia and the Writers Studio in South Boston, and often reads at WAM Poetry Nights and Quarter Day Events in Warrenton, NC. She holds a Master of Arts in Liberal Studies from Hollins University. She is the author of two chapbooks Lady Fingers and The Post Nuptial Agreement. An original One Act Sweeps was a 2024 Page to Stage winner and will be performed on stage in March 2025 at the Kirby Theater and Cultural Arts Complex in Roxboro, NC.

J. Scott Wilson is still organic life from planet Terra (Sol C). He's presently hunched over a computer desk hammering out the finishing touches on an annual poetry journal. He has two of his own books out: *Fist in the Air, Heart on the Ground* and *J. Scott Wilson Gets Carried Away.* He thinks you should buy them. He has brought smiles to the faces of over 75 authors and thinks that's pretty good.

Rabbi Dr. Israel Zoberman is the founder and spiritual leader of Temple Lev Tikvah , and he is the Honorary Senior Rabbi at Eastern Shore Chapel Episcopal Church, both in Virginia Beach, Virginia. He was born in 1945 in Chu, Kazakhstan (USSR) to Polish Holocaust survivors. He spent his early childhood in Poland, Austria and Germany before moving to Israel in 1949. He came to Chicago in 1966. His poetry and translations from Hebrew have been published in CCAR Journal, The Congressional Record, Poetica (guest editor and judge), The Jewish Spectator, The American Rabbi, Moment, and The Poet's Domain, Volumes 5 through 36.

Thank you for your continued support.

Made in the USA
Middletown, DE
11 February 2025

71070898R00055